THIS BOOK BELONGS TO

Turia is an incredible woman. Forthright, fierce, resilient, bold, strong & oozing courage. She has so much to teach us about life, challenges and cultivating confidence. *Good Selfie* is a must read - for you and your kids.

Sandra Sully, Journalist and Senior Editor Ten News

This is the book that every Aussie teen needs to read. Turia is a phenomenal force - her sheer determination, grit and no BS approach to life is outstanding and *Good Selfie* is a must on your bookshelf. It's brimming with lessons and advice about friendships, confidence and how to tackle challenges head on. It should be read by everyone - parents included!

Mia Freedman, Co-founder and Creative Director of the Mamamia Women's Network

Just when I thought she couldn't be any more incredible, Turia Pitt goes and creates *Good Selfie*. This book won't inspire your kids - it will knock their socks off! It's everything Turia is: hilarious, straight-up, deeply moving and wise. If you want your kids to be confident, resilient, kind, well supported and ambitious, this is the book they must read. Congratulations Turia, I couldn't be more proud and inspired by the way you live.

Emma Isaacs, Founder and Global CEO Business Chicks

I met Turia Pitt when we were both judges on the Women's Weekly Women of the Future Awards. Her energy, enthusiasm and intelligence shone in a room full of accomplished women. If you get a chance to meet her or hear from her, grab it!

Leigh Sales, Anchor and Host of ABC's 7.30 Report

Turia Pitt is one tough chick. She's brave, strong, funny and kind - a vibrant person with so much to teach us about living with courage, and smashing big goals. *Good Selfie* is a testament to those qualities and I can't wait to share it with the kids and teens in my life.

Michelle Bridges, Fitness expert and Entrepreneur

Turia Pitt's life story is one of extraordinary strength through her struggle against adversity. Her courage and dignity inspire all people, particularly women and girls. As a national role model we are grateful that she has decided to share with us her emotional and powerful journey.

The Hon Julie Bishop MP, Former Minister for Foreign Affairs

Turia Pitt has never given up. And thank goodness she didn't because she's a terrific human being and someone who's now inspiring thousands of Australians from all walks of life.

Ben Fordham, Journalist and Presenter

I'm continually amazed by this phenomenal woman. Turia Pitt is the living definition of strength, and I can't imagine a better role model for Aussie teens. *Good Selfie* is the book our kids need, and Turia has delivered it with her usual straight-talking wisdom and humour. I can't recommend it enough.

Carrie Bickmore, Co-Host on The Project

Turia is a strong and determined woman. Inspirational in every sense of the word! Put simply, a role model for people of all ages.

Mick Fanning, 3 x Surfing World Champion

Turia, I read your confidence chapter and it helped me so much! You're a rockstar!

– Ashley

Hi Turia, my favourite activities were reframing and negative words and the good words. The book was amazing and really helped me kick some goals out the window. Thank you!

– Elle, 9 years old

If my kids can all take just one of your wonderful life lessons on board during their lifetime, then I'm a happy mum!

– Caroline

The language, questions and tone of the book is fantastic for students as it is written at their level and has been a highly engaging read for students I have used this with.

– Luke, high-school teacher

Turia speaks to kids in their language. My 9 year old absolutely loved this book. I really really recommend buying it – so much wisdom, inspiration and a big wallop of humour too. Thanks for sharing your story with us Turia - and the kids of the future.

– Tammy

Good Selfie is amazing. I read this book knowing that Turia is full of wisdom and great advice. I'm sharing this book with both my 11- and 10-year-old children as Turia is the kind of positive role model I want them looking up to.

– Tarnya

My students are so inspired by your story and it really has made a positive impact on their learning.

– Brendan, high-school teacher

If you've got a teenager in your family or know someone who does, you need to get them onto *Good Selfie*, a book with tips and tools for teens to nail life. I've read it myself and it's bloody brilliant.

– Bel

OTHER COOL STUFF THAT TURIA HAS MADE

Photo credit: Delly Carr

AN INSPIRATIONAL STORY OF TRIUMPH OVER ADVERSITY

UNMASKED
TURIA PITT
AND BRYCE CORBETT

An autobiography 'Unmasked' which has been adapted into a Young Readers' edition.

An epic online program 'School of Champions' to help you smash your goals

mindset magic

five keys to boost your confidence
+ tackle any challenge

An ebook to help you nail your mindset called
(imaginatively 😆) Mindset Magic
....

A baby (what? he counts too!)

TURIA PITT

GOOD SELFIE

TIPS + TOOLS
FOR TEENS TO NAIL LIFE

PLUS A'S TO THE Q'S
I GET ASKED MOST

CONTENTS

Psychologist reviewed

—

Good Selfie has been reviewed by Eliza Vassallo, a registered psychologist and co-founder of Child's Play Qld (a division of a registered Australian charity called the GRT Foundation).

Child's Play Qld seeks to provide high-quality, professional and affordable psychological counselling to children and families. Eliza's long-term vision for the future is that all children, regardless of their family's situation, will be able to come to Child's Play Qld and receive FREE counselling. Eliza's even bigger vision is that the stigma associated with mental health is removed from society and that, instead of shying away from the issues of mental health support, we embrace it and become more vocal and honest as a society about the struggles that we all face and deal with every day.

I pull some hectic facials when I'm speaking.

Having a chinwag with Duchess Kate.

Making coffees when I was 14. I also worked at the local takeaway shop, at the local video shop and at an Italian restaurant. I'm grateful to have had my after-school jobs. They taught me that if I wanted something, I had to work for it.

HEY LEGEND!!

I'm so stoked you're reading this, because, well, I wrote it for you. Not in a creepy stalker-y way! 😂 I wrote it for you and the thousands of kickass teens and kids that I meet every day.

See, as an athlete, author and mindset coach I spend a lot of time travelling and sharing my story with people all over the world. It's interesting because, no matter who I meet, most of my conversations will end the same way – with people asking me how I can be so positive and confident. And it's not just in conversations, I see the same thing again and again in the comments of my Facebook and Instagram posts as well as on Twitter and in the emails I receive every day.

Out of all the questions I get, I really love the ones I receive from teenagers like you. I get asked questions about how to get through tough times and crappy days, questions about confidence and how to smash big goals. So I thought, why not collect a whole bunch of these q&a's and share them around? Maybe my answers and strategies could be helpful for you too!

So that's what *Good Selfie* is, it's a collection of answers to the questions teens ask me most.

I wrote *Good Selfie* because I want to share with you the tools and strategies I used – particularly in my recovery after the fire – to rebuild my life and be my best self.

I'm excited to share them with you.

Because just like there are things to consider when taking the perfect selfie for Instagram (hello lighting and angles!), there are things you can do to create your best, most-confident self in real life.

And just as you'd adjust your camera when taking a selfie, in this book, we'll zoom in and zoom out on some things that will help you form YOUR good selfie.

After all – we only get one shot at life.

This is it. And it's up to YOU to start living the life you want to live.

Let's get stuck in.

Hey, I just met you and this is crazy, but here's my book, read it maybe?

—

Are you wondering who I am and why I've written this book?

Well, let me tell you a little bit about me.

In 2011, I was an ex-model and mining engineer when I was caught in a grassfire while competing in a 100 km ultra-marathon in the Australian outback. I was choppered out of the remote desert barely alive, with full thickness burns to 65 per cent of my body. I lost seven fingers, had over 200 medical procedures and spent two gruelling years in recovery. Surviving against overwhelming odds, I've rebuilt my life and defied every expectation placed on me.

These are some of the things I'm really proud of:

— My beautiful family (Michael and Hakavai)

— I've raised over a million dollars for the charity Interplast

— I've completed two Ironman competitions (including the Ironman World Championships in Kona, Hawaii)

— I've written two bestselling books

— Through sharing my story with the world, I've inspired millions to live with more confidence and smash epic goals.

Now, just to talk myself up even more (geez I'm a bit full of myself hey?!) I've also been shortlisted for Australian of the Year, was a finalist for the Telstra Business Women's Award, and was the winner of the NSW Premier's Woman of the Year.

Through my books, online programs and events, I provide the tools to help you step outside of your comfort zone, kick big goals* and create an EPIC life. More than anything, I aim to be living proof that, with the right attitude to life, we truly can achieve anything.

* Did you follow that asterisk here? Nice work, partner.

Let's talk about goals ... I'm all about setting and getting big goals, but I don't call them that. I call them Champion Quests. Or champies for short. It's probably a silly name but one thing you're gonna need to know about me is that I can be a bit silly. After all, if you can't have a laugh, what's the point?! I call goals 'champies' because, well, I don't know about you, but the word 'goal' always makes me zone out. And champies shouldn't make you snooze! Champies are EPIC, life changing things!

From left to right: Prime minister Scott Morrison, Jenny Morrison, me, Harry and Megs.

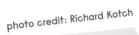

Getting barrelled.

My family.

When I was younger, I used to pretend I was a businesswoman. This is me in my office. I even got Dad to print me business cards!

Hey legend!!

So, what is a champy?

—

A champy is something you really want to achieve for yourself. It's something that excites you, and even makes you a bit nervous because you know there will be lots of hard work involved in achieving it. A champy should stretch you outside your comfort zone and help you to grow.

I'm gonna be talking lots about champies in this book (there's a whole chapter dedicated to 'em), so this is just a heads up that whenever I say champy, what I'm really talking about are goals or dreams - the big things you want to make happen for yourself.

photo credit: Delly Carr

Race day - Ironman World Championships.

Stoked that my book Unmasked is getting read by kids!

photo credit: Salty Dingo

My Dad has always loved Tony Robbins. Was pretty surreal speaking at one of his events and getting a standing ovation from 6000 people!

HOW TO USE
THIS BOOK

Uhhhh, just open it and read it? Hahaha.
No, seriously, it's my hope that you read this book the way YOU want
to read it. You can choose to read it front to back, in one sitting (that's the true
sign of a book nerd – I'd know, I'm one of them!), or you can pick it up, open
to whatever page you want and read what you like.

TL;DR		
	1	At the end of each chapter is a TL;DR section (it looks like this). If your mum is reading this book, tell her that's internet speak for Too Long; Didn't Read!
	2	It's basically a summary of all the key points discussed in each chapter.

Step-by-step activities

—

I've included lots of activities in this book. All of them are exercises that I use in my daily life to help change the way I see my challenges, boost my confidence and create a kickass life. I'm excited for you to get stuck in, but I'd encourage you to go through each activity slowly.

When we try to do too many things at once, it's easy to get overwhelmed. So just take it one step at a time.

What this book is

—

I like to think of it as a guide for living a kickass life, so you can start living life as your best self – your 'good selfie'.

What's this 'good selfie' of yours? Well, that's the you that's brimming with confidence, the you that knows you're capable of big things, the you that faces challenges head on, the you that doesn't let others define who or what you can be.

I've been through a big life changing event and it taught me a lot. I can't wait to share some of these lessons with you; however, I'm not a doctor, and I'm not a psychologist.

What I share with you throughout this book is simply my advice and what worked for me on my journey. Remember to always get a professional opinion and to take on board what makes sense for you and your circumstances.

You do you!

Resources page

—

As you work your way through this book, you'll notice a few references to other websites, guides, activities and resources. To save you trekking all over the internet to find them yourself, I've done you a solid and put everything together on my own website for you!

Wasn't that nice of me?

So, if you want to dive a little deeper into any of the activities or resources I mention throughout the book, just head to:

turiapitt.com/goodselfie-resources

Simple!

1

WHAT IS THE KEY TO YOUR SUCCESS?

I get asked this question allllll the time. I bet you want to know the answer too, yeah? You ready?

It's gratitude.

Now, that's not the only thing that helped me get where I am. All the challenges I've faced and all the goals I've kicked have involved thousands of tiny little moments and steps and parts. But gratitude was, and still is, a major part of my story.

Now, when I give this answer, I can tell that people almost never believe me, because gratitude is so boring, right? But it works. Practising gratitude has been life changing for me.

So, um, what is gratitude?

—

Well, it's being thankful and showing appreciation for everything we have going on in our lives.

Now, when I say gratitude, what do you think of?

I bet you're thinking of barefoot yogis chanting affirmations around a pile of crystals. Right? Or maybe a semi-famous Insta model who's always 'so grateful and blessed' for the opportunity to work with a new diet tea brand?!

Well, if you're into that, more power to you! As always, you do you! But you don't have to be using #blessed on Instagram every day to get the benefits of gratitude.

SIDE NOTE:

People are always looking for those little 'secret keys' to success aren't they? Whether they want to get fit, make money, get smart – everyone wants to do it and do it FAST. But the reality is, magic pills and quick fixes don't work in the long run.

Success in any form usually means hard work, sacrifice and, yes, a whole lot of gratitude practised along the way. And I reckon the lessons learned the hard way are always the most important.

If it feels hard, congratulations, that means you're getting somewhere!

I bang on about gratitude for a reason

—

Why? Well, it's hard to feel good about yourself and achieve the things you want most when you're feeling negative, angry, bitter, jealous or confused. You can't kick big goals when you're feeling and thinking negative thoughts.

And gratitude is one of the best ways to short-circuit those kinds of thoughts and feelings.

Because when you're truly grateful that's the only emotion you'll feel. Think about it - it's impossible to be grateful and angry at the same time, or grateful and bitter at the same time.

This is important to know:

Gratitude is not something you just have, it's something you do.

It's a skill, and it's one you can practise right now.

On the following pages there's a collection of my a's to q's about gratitude plus a stack of gratitude activities for you to get stuck into.

My advice for the activities is to pick one, just one, and try it for a week. If it doesn't work, that's ok, try another one!

Q

Was there a time when practising gratitude really helped you deal with negative thoughts?

— Sam, 14

A

I had to draw on a whole stack of mindset strategies to get me through the Ironman World Championships, but hands down, gratitude was the tool I came back to time and time (and time!) again.

When I didn't think I could take another step, I'd think about everything in my life I was grateful for – the people who had helped me get to that moment, the ability to use my body, the other competitors driving me to be my best.

The feeling of gratitude for all of that helped me to keep moving and to keep pushing to finish the race.

It's pretty amazing because before the fire, just five years earlier, I'd never even really thought about gratitude.

It's not that I was ungrateful, just like I know you're not, but I never actively practised gratitude.

I was too caught up in the idea of all the things I still had to achieve, all the things that my life wasn't yet.

But when you flip that – when you start to express gratitude for what you have and what you are right now?

Well, in my experience, that's how you form the foundations of an epic life.

Q

How do you practise gratitude?

— Lisa, 16

A

The way I practise gratitude daily is pretty simple.
Every morning, as soon as I wake up, I take a few minutes
just to think of three things I'm grateful for.

I try to be as specific as possible.

So, instead of thinking 'I'm grateful for my mum', I'll try
to think about something I'm really specifically grateful for,
like 'I'm grateful for the time Mum spent with me yesterday
helping me fix my surfboard' or 'I'm grateful for my partner
Michael for making dinner last night'.

It's such a simple exercise but it really sets you up for a day
full of that gratitude attitude.

If you want, you can level this up by setting gratitude alerts
in your phone.

Set reminders to go off at different times of the day,
and when one goes off, think of three things you're grateful
for in that moment.

I also find that music helps me get into that gratitude zone.
I made a gratitude playlist for myself (and for you!) on
Spotify, so if you're keen you can check out page 19.

Q

What are you grateful for and why?

— Matthew, 13

A

I'm grateful for all kinds of things!

But today, I'm grateful for living by the ocean because it allows me to surf often, which I love. I'm also grateful for Michael, for always catching and cooking me delicious fish, and for my dad for helping me with a speech last week.

Q

I heard you say once that you were grateful for the fire ... is that true? If so, why?

— Miranda, 17

A

Yep, believe it or not, I am grateful for the fire. Yeah, I'd never want to re-live what I went through in recovery, and I wouldn't wish that experience on anyone, but I'm still grateful for it.

No one has the power to change the past.

But you can be grateful for the lessons the past teaches you.

Because of what I've been through I know that I can get through hard times and I know that I'm capable of anything I put my mind to.

That's what tough times teach us.

IMPORTANT WORDS UP THERE

DO

GRATITUDE

READY TO START GETTING THAT GRATITUDE ATTITUDE?

Get started with my gratitude challenges
on the following pages!

CHALLENGE ONE

REFLECT

(AND NOT IN A MIRROR!
ON PAPER, YOU GOOSE!)

I want you to use the space below to list all of the things in your life that you've made happen. Successes! Wins! Things that you're proud of.

Maybe you aced an exam at school, scored the winning try at a footy game last season or finally perfected that pancake recipe. Whatever it is, big or small, if you're proud of it ...

WRITE IT DOWN:

Now, use the space below here to write a list of your strengths.

Maybe you're a great listener, good at spelling, a good cook, super co-ordinated – whatever you consider a strength

WRITE IT DOWN:
_____

THEY SEE ME ROLLIN', REFLECTIN'

Now I want you to reflect on these two lists. Allow yourself to feel proud of your achievements and feel gratitude for the skills and strengths that made them happen.

Now for the last step:

I want you to write a letter to yourself (hear me out!) expressing gratitude for your strengths and your successes - all the things about yourself that you're proud of (you can check out my letter by going to the link on page 19).

WRITE IT HERE, WITH A PEN. GO ON, GET WRITING!

CHALLENGE TWO

SHARE

ONE

Think about the people in your life that you're grateful for.

WRITE THEIR NAMES DOWN BELOW.

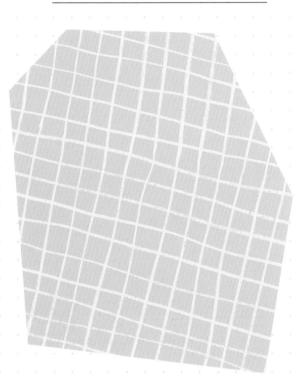

TWO

Tell these people that you're grateful for them and why - and be specific.

FOR EXAMPLE

Don't just thank your friend for being your friend! Thank them for helping you with your maths homework last week or for taking you to that concert.

Being specific allows you to really understand WHY you're grateful for that person. And on the flip side, it feels good when people recognise you and express thanks for your actions.

SIDE NOTE:

Why do I want you to handwrite this stuff?

Well, handwriting creates wayyyyy more neural pathways in your brain than typing does - typing only uses eight different movements while handwriting uses up to 10,000!

What does that mean? Well, in a nutshell, it means that our brain values what we handwrite more than what we type. So, if it's important, handwrite it!

Pretty cool, huh?

1 —— Gratitude

CHALLENGE THREE

PUT IT OUT THERE

ONE   Reach out to an author, musician, teacher, or anyone who has had a positive impact on you and thank them.

TWO   Take a photo of something you're grateful for and post it to Instagram, Facebook or Twitter and tag it with #GoodSelfie, #GratitudeAttitude and @turiapitt so I can see what you're grateful for.

PS. I know it's scary sharing part of yourself with strangers. But being open and vulnerable is how we grow, and that's what you're here on this planet to do!

TL;DR

1	Gratitude is not something you have, it's something you do. It's something you need to practise.
2	When you're truly grateful, that's the only emotion you'll experience.
3	No one has the power to change the past. But you can be grateful for the lessons the past teaches you.
4	Being open and vulnerable is how we grow.

2

GOT CONFI— DENCE?

Ahhhh, confidence. The secret key to life that everyone wants.
I could talk about this for days. But to save you that (aren't you lucky?!),
I've picked three questions that I get asked a lot, and answered them
for you here. I hope they help you to build your self-confidence.

Q

I don't look like
any of the girls
I see on Instagram
and every time
I think about
it I feel like crap ...

— Katie, 15

Katie, do you wanna know what I am constantly asked?

It's 'How are you so confident?'.

Now, I know people don't mean that in a nasty way, quite the opposite, but what they're really asking is how I can be so confident when I look so *different*.

There's this perception that the 'better' we look, the more confidence we'll have.

Now, there's nothing wrong with caring about how you look. I'll be the first to tell you that I love looking my best. I love rocking fresh threads and I'm still trying to find ways to talk myself out of many a purchase at the Mecca Beauty counter. I'll also always explore new medical advancements that will help me smooth my skin and improve my appearance.

But what that boils down to is having pride in my appearance.

If I rocked up to a speaking gig with my teeth not brushed, wearing ugg boots and my PJs, I wouldn't feel confident to speak in front of thousands of people! However, if I've exercised that morning, if I've taken pride in my appearance and put my best foot forward, I'm going to feel more capable and therefore more confident.

There's nothing wrong with presenting the best version of yourself to the world. But don't fall into the massive trap of thinking that you have to look a certain way or look like some airbrushed Insta girl to feel confident.

Because confidence is made up of LOTS of different things. Yes, appearance might be one facet. But it's not the only one!

Those girls on Instagram are using FILTERS. Heard of them?! Remember: You can't compare your behind-the-scenes with someone else's highlights reel! To the right is a selfie I took one day when I was hanging around the house with Michael. Below is a pic taken with my hair and makeup done, a team of stylists and a photographer behind the lens, professional lighting and some filters at work. What you see on Instagram isn't always reality.

NO MAKEUP SELFIE

PORTRAIT WITH JUST A SMIDGE OF MAKEUP + STYLING...

ONE MORE THING:

If looking at someone's social media feed makes you feel bad about yourself, unfollow them ASAP. Like, right now. What are you doing? Put this book down and go and unfollow them!

OK, it's time for a little flashback

—

(cue the wavy pictures, wind chimes and soft lighting) Before the fire, I was a super-confident person. I was athletic, I had a good job, I had an awesome boyfriend, I had a big circle of friends, I raised money for charities.

I was killing it and my confidence was sky high.

And then the fire came along and changed everything. I found myself in a hospital bed with my physical abilities completely stripped away.

I was made redundant from my job, I was socially isolated (my friends were all off working and travelling the ✈ world, and I was stuck in rehab), I was forced to wear a compression mask that made me stick out like a sore thumb, my boyfriend became my carer and I was completely dependant on him and my mum to do the most basic of tasks.

I also lost pride in my appearance - I would wear Michael's t-shirts and track pants with crocs 👟 (stylish, I know) and Michael would have to brush my hair on the rare occasion that I let him!

Instead of spending my weekends rock climbing in gorges with Michael, I was spending my weeks at rehab centres and was constantly in and out of operating theatres.

So, yep, as you can imagine, I wasn't feeling confident.

BEFORE THE FIRE

DURING RECOVERY

TODAY

credit: Juli Balla

So, how'd you get it back?

—

I had to slowly rebuild my ability to do the things
that made me feel confident: running, ∿ surfing,
challenging myself physically, raising money for charities,
studying, reading and getting smarter.

I also started taking pride in my appearance again -
I started brushing my hair, wearing cool gym outfits and
painting my toenails 💅.

All of these 'little things' came together and slowly,
my confidence grew and grew.

I've got a q for you:

—

How do you measure your confidence right now?
Is it just tied up in how you look? What about your respect*
for yourself, your sporting abilities, how smart you are
in class, what a great friend you are, how you help
your community?

On the next page is a cool little circle that shows all
the ways in which I feel confident. It looks a little like a pie
chart, which is why I call it my Confidence Pie (yum?!).

* When I say self-respect I mean how you treat yourself. Are you kind to yourself, do you look after
yourself, do you take pride in your appearance and pride in your abilities?

DANGER!

Do you get a little ego boost
whenever one of your pics does well
on Instagram or social media?
That's ok (I get it - that happens
to me too!) but it can't be the only
way you feel good about yourself.
One of the dangers is that you're
relying on what other people think
about you to make you feel good,
and your confidence has got
to come from within.

CONFIDENCE PIE

Here it is, my delicious little Confidence Pie!

See how I draw confidence from lots of different things?

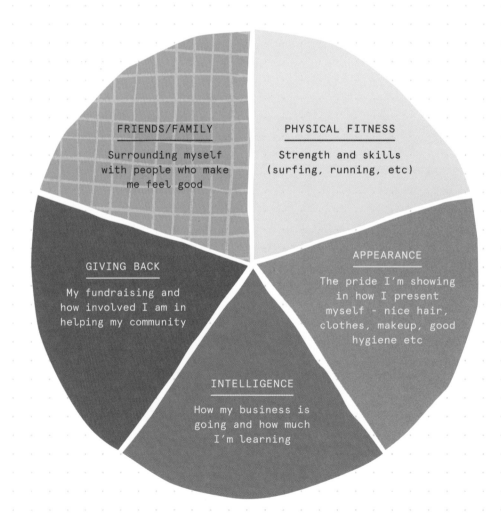

FRIENDS/FAMILY

Surrounding myself with people who make me feel good

PHYSICAL FITNESS

Strength and skills (surfing, running, etc)

APPEARANCE

The pride I'm showing in how I present myself - nice hair, clothes, makeup, good hygiene etc

GIVING BACK

My fundraising and how involved I am in helping my community

INTELLIGENCE

How my business is going and how much I'm learning

YOUR TURN

I want you to think about all the things that help you to feel more confident and add them to the blank circle to create your own Confidence Pie!

EXAMPLES:

Maybe you feel your confidence grow when you're playing footy, studying, preparing for a debate, getting your hair braided or raising money for your school?

Remember, this is YOUR Confidence Pie, so be honest with yourself about the things that really make YOU feel confident, not what you think 'should' make you feel confident.

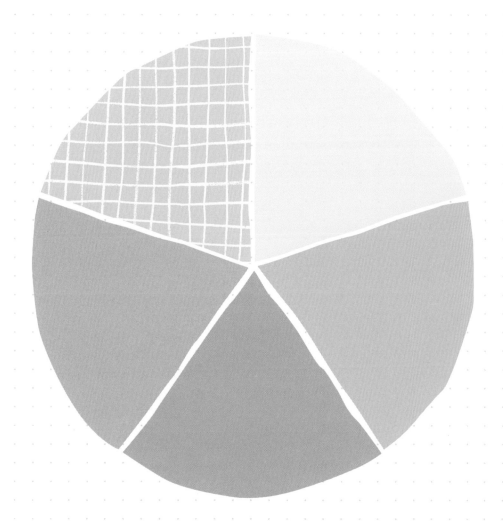

Q

What can I do to be confident like you?

—Hayley, 14

A

As your Confidence Pie will show you, Hayley, confidence starts with YOU.

I have some q's for you:

How do you treat your body? Do you fuel up with good food, get enough sleep and move daily? (And when I say 'move' that can be anything from walking, swimming and surfing to playing footy and dancing - whatever! Just move that body.)

What words do you use to describe yourself? Do you look at yourself in the mirror, pinch your stomach and tell yourself you're disgusting? Or do you smile at yourself and say 'Good morning sunshine!'?

(Psst: check out the self talk chapter on page 62 for more on this.)

What are your personal relationships like? Do they make you feel good about yourself? Or do the people you spend time with bring you down?

See, feeling confident is easier when you're healthy and strong, hanging with people who make you feel great, and being kind to yourself.

Start building healthy habits in these areas and your confidence will start to skyrocket.

But, here's an important tip - just pick ONE area to work on first. When you try to do too many things at once, it's easy to get overwhelmed.

Maybe you can start with drinking more water, walking every day, or getting more sleep? Once that becomes a habit, you can pick something else to work on. Simple!

Wanna break this down even more?

—

Have you ever noticed that after you make a mistake, say the wrong thing or put your foot in your mouth (not literally of course, unless you're an ex-Olympic gymnast! 😂), you ask yourself questions like 'Why am I such an idiot?', 'Why do I always stuff up?' or 'Why can't I do anything right?'.

In our brain, we have what's called the RAS – the Reticular Activating System (bear with me here – that's as science-y as I'm gonna get, I promise).

The RAS is basically a mini Google inside your head. So, when you ask yourself a question, it's like typing that question straight into your internal Google search bar.

Whatever you search for, you'll find.

So, if you wanted to buy a cool pair of kicks, you'll start to notice the ones you want everywhere. Your RAS presents evidence for the things you think about or ask questions about.

Likewise, if you make a mistake in an exam and immediately ask yourself a crappy question like, 'Why am I such an idiot?' your brain will start searching for evidence to prove that you're an idiot! All of a sudden you'll start thinking about all the other times you've messed up.

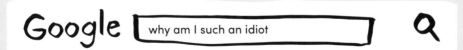

Your RAS doesn't discriminate

—

Google │ what can i learn from this? │ Q

It will just find the answers to the questions you ask. So if you ask yourself a better question like, 'What can I learn from this?' – your brain will start the search and come up with answers that are more helpful. Something like 'Maybe next time I can get someone to help me revise for that exam'.

Your mindset is critical for failure or success. And part of the shift in mindset is simply asking yourself better questions.

Q

You always seem
so confident.
Do you ever have
days when you feel
self-conscious?

—Tim, 16

A

Everyone feels self-conscious sometimes - even footy stars, models, neurosurgeons, presidents and pro-surfers. It doesn't matter how attractive people find you, how smart you are or how good you are at something - no one is immune to feeling unconfident and self-conscious.

It's ok to feel self-conscious sometimes.

On the days I feel self-conscious, I have three options available to me:

ONE I can choose to just accept it and wallow for a while. (Wallowing means letting yourself really feel whatever it is you're feeling.) I decide to just let myself feel uncertain and a bit down. That's ok. But I usually give myself a time limit, otherwise I can find myself feeling bad for a whole day!

So, I give myself an hour just to feel it, and then I go and do something that makes me feel better.

TWO I do something that makes me feel good. I have a list of things that always make me feel positive. It includes: going for a surf, reading a good book, hanging out with mates, going for a run.

All of those things make me feel positive and in charge.

THREE The third option is for those times when, for whatever reason, I can't wallow OR do something to make me feel better. In those cases, I just have to OWN IT.

I'll give you an example.

I remember this time I had to travel for a speech. It was just a few days after I'd had laser surgery on my skin, which makes my face and neck really red and sore. I was walking through the airport and, maybe it was just my imagination, but I just felt like everyone was staring at me.

To be honest with you, I started to get upset. But you know what? Sometimes, you've just gotta remind yourself that no one else's opinion or judgement matters. And so I thought to myself 'Stuff it! You've gotta own this like a boss'.

Because, here's the thing:

If you can't own yourself, no one else is gonna do it for you.

—

So, maybe you feel self-conscious right before you walk into an exam. You can't head out to throw the footy around or watch a funny movie, and you can't afford to wallow because that might affect your performance. That's a time when you've gotta just put your chin up, act brave and confident and OWN IT.

PS. There's a TED talk by Amy Cuddy that I really love. It's all about how your body language can help you feel more confident. So, pulling your shoulders back and acting brave will actually make you feel brave! Check it out on page 19.

That day at the airport

—

 turiapitt ✓ • Follow

turiapitt I've been recovering from laser surgery for the past week. Sometimes I get really self-conscious after surgery - I feel like everyone is having a huge stickybeak at me. This week I felt it big time, and yeah, it sucks. But you know what? Sometimes in life when you're on a quest to improve yourself, no one else's opinion or judgement matters. You've gotta own yourself and wear your challenges like a boss - after all, no one else is gonna do it for you!

Load more comments

beautifulladythia You are a true inspiration and definitely motivation. Bless you!

the_siren_athena You have a good heart

jenyrde 👍🖤

mal_asia 🖤🖤

rociomichunovich @hachikubomartu

I even went so far as to post a selfie on social media (check it above). I'm not suggesting you have to post a photo next time you get a big pimple or cold sore and feel self-conscious about it, I just want you to know that the world doesn't end every time you feel self-conscious. You're gonna be ok.

People can be mean. People do judge - we can all judge sometimes. You can't control that.

So you need to focus on what you can control - your reaction. Pull your shoulders back and own it like a boss. So, to answer your q, Tim, when you feel self-conscious you've got three options:

ONE Allow yourself an hour to feel it, then move on.

TWO Do something that makes you feel good.

THREE Own it.

TL;DR

1	Confidence comes from a lot more than just what we look like.
2	Confidence begins with YOU. Look after yourself, and work on making your self talk POSITIVE.
3	You'll always find what you're looking for, so start looking for the positive.
4	Feeling insecure? Wallow for an hour, do something fun or own it like a boss!
5	Everyone feels self-conscious sometimes, and that's ok.

3

LET'S TALK ABOUT UM, TALK?

Self talk, actually. What's self talk?
Well, it's the way you think about yourself and the way you speak to yourself
inside your head. This is such a BIGGIE. The words we use have so much
power. Whatever we think - our brain creates. So if you're constantly using
words that bring yourself down, well guess how you're gonna feel?
(Hint: it's not up!) Let's dive into this some more. On the next page, I've got
a self talk challenge that might just change the game for you.

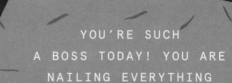

CHALLENGE

I've got a challenge for you. For the next week, I want you to start paying attention to how you speak to yourself and how you describe yourself to others. Look out for words that don't make you feel so crash hot.

FOR EXAMPLE:

I'm really careful about the words I use to describe myself. Can you see how the terms 'burns victim' and 'disfigured' are more negative than 'burns survivor' and 'different'?

So, whether it's saying it out loud or talking to myself in my own head, I never use words that make me feel bad about myself.

I would never describe myself as 'disfigured'. And if other people use that word, I gently remind them that no, I'm not disfigured – I just look a bit different.

I want you to have a really honest think about the words you use to describe yourself.

What words make you feel bad? Could you replace them with more positive ones?

Try and think of a few examples of your own, and what words you could use instead. Use the spaces on the next page to write them down.

It's a small and simple switch but it packs a huge punch.

OLD, NEGATIVE WORDS

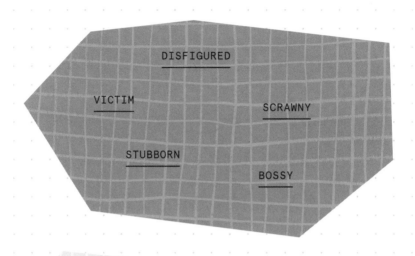

DISFIGURED

VICTIM

SCRAWNY

STUBBORN

BOSSY

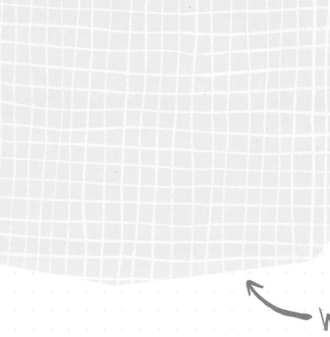

WRITE HERE

NEW, FEEL-GOOD WORDS

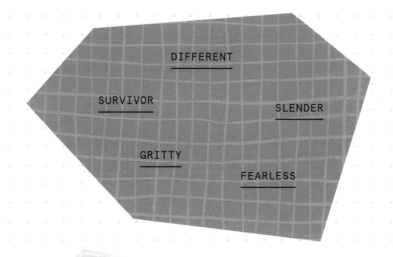

DIFFERENT
_____

SURVIVOR
_____

SLENDER
_____

GRITTY
_____

FEARLESS
_____

AND HERE ⟶

Q

I always feel like I'm failing at things. How do I change that?

— Krista, 15

Krista, I've got a q for you:

Have you ever actually listened to the conversations you have with yourself? More importantly, have you noticed the mean stuff you say to yourself?

For example, maybe you make a mistake and you think 'You're so stupid, you never do anything right'.

That right there is your inner critic speaking.

You might recognise your inner critic from such films as 'I'm A Stupid Failure', 'I'm Fat and Ugly', 'No One Will Ever Like Me' and 'I'm Going To Fail School'.

Sound familiar?! That's the kind of self talk you've gotta change.

After all, how are you supposed to feel good about yourself if you're constantly thinking about the things you do and say in a negative way?

The good news? You're 100% in charge of your inner critic and you CAN shut that chat down.

On the next page, I've listed three of my favourite strategies for battling my inner critic.

This week, try to take notice of any mean chat from your inner critic and then use my tips to shut it down. Worth a shot yeah?

HOW TO:

WIN THE BATTLE AGAINST YOUR INNER CRITIC

ONE

Start talking to yourself like you would to your best mate. You'd never say 'you're a failure' or 'you're a loser' to someone you love! So why say that to yourself?

TWO

Use a silly voice! Change your inner critic's voice into a silly voice. This works for me every time.

HERE'S HOW YOU DO IT:

Every time you notice your inner critic throwing you an insult, catch it, and then repeat it out loud using a silly accent or character voice. I always use Homer Simpson's voice but you could have a crack at a Dobby or Darth Vader voice!

Yes, you'll look and sound like a bit of a dork, but the point is, when you hear that insult in a different voice, you realise just how silly it is and that it doesn't deserve to take up any more of your headspace.

THREE

List small wins. Every time I felt like I just wasn't getting anywhere in my recovery after the fire, I would think of three small things that I'd done well that day.

FOR EXAMPLE:

— I'd done really well in my physio session

— I took my mask off for a full hour around friends

— I helped Michael put the clothes on the line

So, next time you feel like you're failing, try thinking about three times you've actually been a winner. Maybe you got to school on time, did your best on an assignment, and helped out a bit around the house. Celebrate every achievement - even the smallest ones.

CHANGE YOUR THOUGHTS AND YOU'LL CHANGE YOUR WORLD

— NORMAN VINCENT PEALE

Q

What do you do when you're just not feeling happy about yourself?

— Josh, 17

A

If I'm not feeling very happy about myself, there are five things I try to do:

ONE I try to look at the reasons WHY I'm not happy. If it's because I made a big mistake at work, I'll try to see if there's something I can learn from that mistake. Maybe there's something I can change or something I can improve on? I always see if there's a way I can GROW from the experience.

TWO I accept that I'm not gonna be happy all the time. It's not realistic to expect that we're always gonna be super happy. Just as we have good days, we have ok days and we have bad days too. So, I just accept the bad days and think: 'Ok, today isn't the greatest. That's all right. Tomorrow is a new day and I'll probably feel better then.'

THREE Use a mantra. I picked up this tip from a really cool chick named Katie Piper (look her up!). In hospital, I had a lot of bad days. Whenever I felt unhappy about my situation I would repeat this phrase over and over:

'I may feel bad today but I won't always feel this way.'

Use the space on the next page to come up with your own mantra, or try using mine. It sounds a bit cray-cray but it worked for me.

MY MANTRA

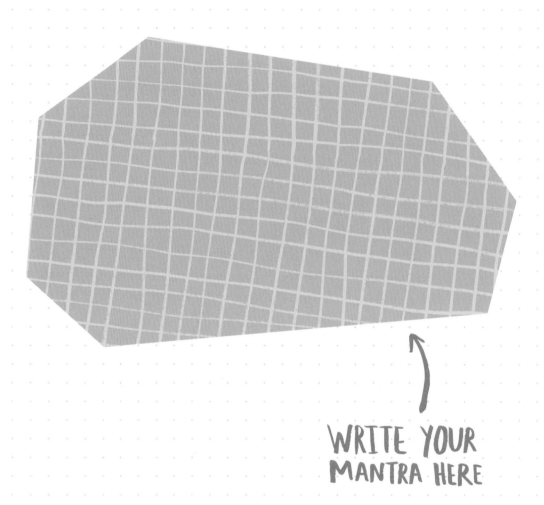

WRITE YOUR
MANTRA HERE

FOUR

I also look for 'happy tokens' throughout the day. What's a happy token? It's just you noticing and appreciating happy moments. The cool thing is, by looking for happy tokens, you're rewiring your brain to focus on the positives rather than the negatives.

If I'm feeling unhappy about myself, I'll start looking for three happy tokens. This could be a good book I'm reading, a baby smiling at me, or the fact that my favourite song came on the radio.

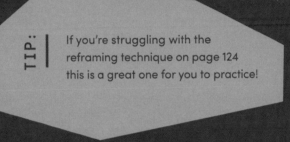

TIP:

If you're struggling with the reframing technique on page 124 this is a great one for you to practice!

FIVE

When you're feeling unhappy about yourself, it's even more important to have a little TLC!

If you don't take care of yourself (eating great food that's good for you, making sure you exercise, spending time with your friends and family, getting enough sleep), everything feels harder.

YO, THIS IS IMPORTANT

Remember, no one is super happy
all the time. Just as we have

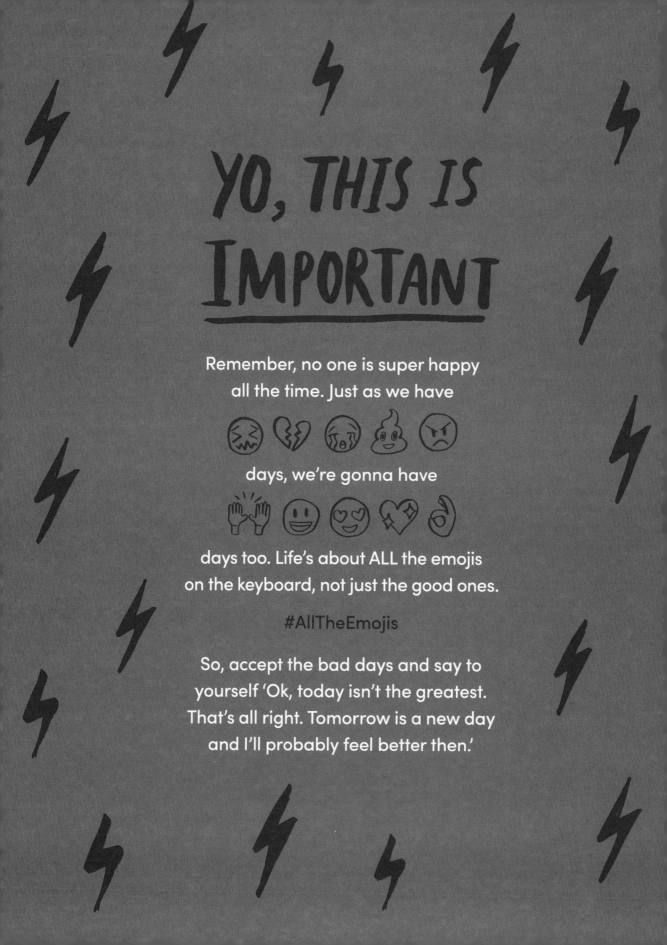

days, we're gonna have

days too. Life's about ALL the emojis
on the keyboard, not just the good ones.

#AllTheEmojis

So, accept the bad days and say to
yourself 'Ok, today isn't the greatest.
That's all right. Tomorrow is a new day
and I'll probably feel better then.'

Mirror, mirror on the wall ... ummmm, yeah, how is she so g-damn perfect all the time?
—

Remember your inner critic? (I know, who'd want to?!) Well, I always find that it's when I compare myself to other people that my inner critic goes into overdrive. That negative self talk takes over and, before long, I end up feeling like crap.

Issy knows what I'm talking about! Check out her question on the next page.

Q

I always compare myself to everyone else and feel worse. What should I do?

— Issy, 14

A

Issy, this is so normal, and it's a trap that almost everyone falls into.

The antidote? Gratitude.

Whenever I find myself comparing my appearance, fitness level, intelligence, physical ability or even just my stuff to someone else's, I immediately practise gratitude.

I remember when I got to Kona, Hawaii for the Ironman World Championships, I'd go out training and everywhere I looked, I'd see all these crazy-fit people with insanely strong, lean bodies and all this fancy gear and I'd feel sick.

I'd think: 'How the hell am I supposed to compete alongside these guys?! They're professionals. You shouldn't even be here Turia.'

I'd catch myself thinking this way and just feel so bad. So, to stop this mean chat, I started practising gratitude (turn to page 32 for all my fave gratitude activities). Within minutes I'd be back in control of my thoughts and feeling so much more positive. The experience taught me to, quite literally, focus on my own race.

You've got to stay in your lane. Don't worry about what other people are doing.

Focus on yourself, and on keeping your self talk positive.

BTW

Social media has the power to send your inner critic
into CRAZY levels of overdrive – whether it's comparing
yourself to others or getting that major FOMO.

Have a quick think about how you're feeling just before
you jump on social media, and then check in with how
you feel after. A lot of people say they feel worse.
I'm not saying get off social altogether (that would
be hypocritical because I'm on Instagram a lot!),
but maybe give this tip a try ...

Change up your social feeds so you start seeing
heaps of posts from people who inspire you, make you
feel good about yourself, make you laugh or help
you 'zoom out' and get some perspective. Chuck them
a like or comment so you keep seeing more of them
in your feed.

Try following
@kurtfearnley @emmawatson @bethanyhamilton
@serenawilliams @nationalgeographic
and duh! @turiapitt.

Also if looking at someone's feed makes you feel
bad about yourself, derrrrrrr, unfollow them stat!

COMPARISON IS THE THIEF OF JOY

— THEODORE ROOSEVELT

Q

How hard is it to do everyday things? Are there things you still can't do?

— Bailey, 14

A

Every skill I have now is a skill I've had to re-learn. Things like brushing my hair, doing up my jeans, cutting up my food (with seven fingers gone) – I had to re-learn all of those things.

There's a quote by Marie Forleo that I really love:

'Everything is figureoutable'.

If something is important to me, I'll figure out a way to do it. So, learning to tie my shoelaces was important to me because I love running. Learning to surf well again is something I'm dedicating lots of time to, because that's a skill that's really important to me.

Learning new skills takes time so I want to use my time re-learning the skills that matter most to me. Whenever I find something difficult, I remind myself that, just like any new skill, it's gonna take time before I'll be able to do it easily.

My mum actually taught me this. In hospital, whenever I got angry about not being able to do something, I'd say 'I can't do this'. My mum would immediately say 'Turia, you can't do this YET'.

Just by adding those three little letters 'YET' to the end of that statement, I was reminded that just because I couldn't do something at the time, it didn't mean I wouldn't be able to find a way to make it happen in the future.

So, when you're finding things hard, try making that switch. Instead of saying 'I can't do this', try saying 'I can't do this yet'.

YOUR
HAPPINESS
DEPENDS ON YOU;
NO ONE CAN
'MAKE YOU HAPPY'
...THAT'S YOUR JOB

— TURIA PITT

TL;DR

1	The way you talk to and about yourself has a massive impact on how you feel. You need to challenge your inner critic; don't just accept what he/she says as true.
2	Don't expect to be happy all the time. It's not possible for any of us, and that's ok. Remember ... life's about #AllTheEmojis
3	Comparing yourself to other people on social media or IRL can send your negative self talk into a spiral. The key to breaking out of that headspace is gratitude.
4	Take responsibility for your own happiness - start a gratitude practice, change up your social media feed, get a mantra, list out your small wins.

4

GOALS

**So, you wanna know the most common question I get asked? It's this:
How did you do it? How did you manage to rebuild your life? How did you
manage to bounce back from such hard times? How did you overcome all
those setbacks?**

Yep, I get it in all variations, but
essentially it's the same thing:
people want to know how I faced
big, painful, major challenges and
came out the other side.

And just for you, I'm gonna share
my secret:

G O A L S.

But you know, I don't call them
goals. I call them champies!

No idea what I'm on about?
Check out the intro of this book

(page 14) for more. Yep, the things
that kept me going, the things that
kept me trying to improve, were
my champies. They were crucial
to my recovery and I wouldn't be
where I am today without them.

I love the champy-chasing process.
Why? Because when you set a
champy, one that scares and excites
you and pushes you way outside
your comfort zone - and then you
do the work to achieve it - you learn
a whole heap about yourself.

Photo credit: Michael Klein

CHAMPIES :

- ✓ INCREASE YOUR CONFIDENCE

- ✓ GROW YOUR RESILIENCE (YOUR ABILITY
  TO HANDLE THE TOUGH TIMES)

- ✓ BUILD YOUR SELF-ESTEEM (THE WAY YOU
  THINK AND FEEL ABOUT YOURSELF)

- ✓ BUILD MOMENTUM

What do I mean by momentum? Well, achieving something that really matters to you has a flow-on effect to the rest of your life. It gets the ball rolling.

If you work hard to achieve your champy of getting on the State Netball Team or getting a lead role in the school play, suddenly the idea of smashing your final school exams doesn't seem so crazy. Because now you have proof that you are capable of the hard work required to get you there.

That's a really powerful thing to realise about yourself, and that's the momentum created by goal getting/champy chasing.

I'm living proof that we can achieve anything we put our minds to. And when you understand and really believe that, it is INCREDIBLE the direction your life can take. In this chapter, I want to answer some q's that relate, in different ways, to champy chasing. I hope my a's help you to smash your biggest champies too!

Q

What motivated you to get better?

— Amanda, 16

A

To be honest, I think my initial motivation came from my stubbornness. I've got a little streak of rebellion in me that makes me want to prove other people wrong.

So when a doctor told me, early on in my recovery, that it was unlikely I'd ever run again, it was like a light bulb lit up in my head. I remember thinking 'I'll show you. I'm gonna do an Ironman one day'.

Now, at the time I had no idea what an Ironman was; I just thought it was the guy on the back of the Nutri-Grain box! But I knew it was the ultimate test in fitness, and even though I couldn't even stand up by myself, I distinctly remember this overwhelming desire to prove everyone wrong and complete an Ironman.

So that was my motivation.

When it comes to setting champies, you've gotta have a clear idea of what you're trying to achieve (also known as your 'what') and you've gotta have a really clear and specific reason to achieve it (also known as your 'why').

My 'why' was really clear and really compelling.

Because of my injuries, people lowered their expectations of what they thought I could achieve. I wanted to prove to them, and to myself, that I could become fitter, faster and stronger than I was before the fire.

So, whatever champy you might want to achieve, try to get really clear on why it is you want to achieve it.

Maybe you want to do really well in your final school exams so you can get into a Veterinary Science degree and fulfil your lifelong dream of helping animals.

Maybe you want to start a blog or YouTube channel to kickstart the career in music you dream about.

Maybe you want to live in a treehouse with 64 cats because you like treehouses and cats?! 🐱 🐱 🐱

Hey, you do you!

ACTIVITY

I want you to think about something you want to achieve. Something you've ALWAYS wanted to achieve but, for whatever reason, haven't been able to yet.

Got something in mind?

OK, WRITE IT DOWN BELOW.

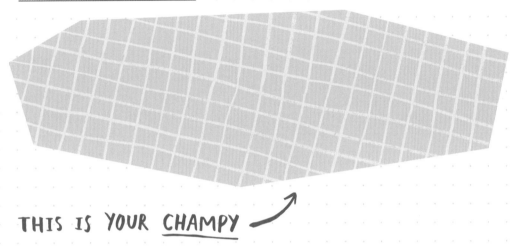

THIS IS YOUR CHAMPY ⟶

Now, answer me this: is your champy specific? What I mean is, if you want to get into that Vet Science degree, did you write down 'Achieve a mark over XXX in my final exams and get accepted into a Vet Science degree at XXXX University' or did you write down 'Do well in my exams'?

When you're specific with your champy, that helps your brain really understand what is required to get there.

USE THE SPACE BELOW TO RE-WRITE YOUR CHAMPY,

MAKING IT AS SPECIFIC AS POSSIBLE.

NOW, YOU READY TO GO OUT THERE AND SMASH THAT CHAMPY?

Ok,ok, hold your horses.

Just answer me one thing first:

WHY DO YOU WANT TO ACHIEVE IT?
_____

Having a clear and compelling reason for achieving your champy is SO important.
If you don't have a compelling reason, I can guarantee you that you won't be able to follow through.

You'll need to remember your 'why' time and time again when the going gets tough (and trust me, it's gonna get tough at some point).

The more reasons you can come up with, the more likely it is that you'll achieve what you're chasing.

If you already have a compelling reason to achieve your champy, awesome!

WRITE IT DOWN BELOW:
_____

NEED A HAND ANSWERING THOSE Q's?

WHAT IS YOUR CHAMPY?

I WANT TO MAKE THE NETBALL TEAM.

But, remember, we've gotta be more specific than that!

WHAT IS YOUR CHAMPY, SPECIFICALLY?

I WANT TO IMPROVE MY GOAL-SHOOTING TECHNIQUE SO MUCH THAT I MAKE THE TEAM GOING TO NEW ZEALAND FOR THE NETBALL CHAMPIONSHIPS.

WHY DO YOU WANT TO ACHIEVE THIS?

IT WOULD GIVE ME MORE PRIDE IN MYSELF AND IN MY SCHOOL. IT WOULD HELP ME BECOME MORE CONFIDENT AND COME OUT OF MY SHELL A BIT. IT WOULD INTRODUCE ME TO A WHOLE NEW CIRCLE OF FRIENDS THAT I HAVE SOMETHING IN COMMON WITH. AND IT WOULD PROBS GIVE ME SOME CRED TOO!

Q

Did you ever want to just give up because it was too hard? How did you keep going?

— Grace, 14

A

Yep, of course. I had lots of low moments and bad days when it all just seemed too hard.

I remember one day in particular. It was not long after the fire and I was learning how to stand up on my own again.

I'd just come out of my coma, I was still burnt raw and it was excruciating for me to make the slightest movement.

Each breath that I took felt as if a thick layer of skin was getting peeled off me but it was super important to my doctors that they got me moving as soon as possible.

So four physios came into my room to help me to stand.

There were two physios on either side of my hospital bed, one behind me supporting my head and neck, and one was in front of me almost pulling me to my feet.

I could hear my pulse through my heart rate monitor and it was through the roof.

That moment was the hardest moment of my whole life. Not because of the pain but because, at that moment, I realised how long my recovery would be.

I'd been burnt running in a 100 kilometre race. Now I didn't even have the strength to get myself out of bed.

Forget Ironman! How was I gonna be able to walk, run, go back to work, surf, have a family with Michael?

I came to realise that if I only focused on the idea of getting my life back, I would have always felt like giving up.

Why? Because the gap between where I was and where I wanted to be was gigantic.

I realised that all I could do was focus on one tiny step at a time.

So, that's what I did. I focused on all the tiny steps along the way. I'd aim to walk three laps of the hallway, then a flight of stairs, then all the stairs up to the Burns Unit.

By focusing on the small steps, I was able to build my confidence and stay motivated.

Maybe you've felt the same before? Maybe there's something you want to achieve that feels just way too big, almost impossible?

Try breaking it up into smaller steps and get working towards the first one, and then the next, and the next and the next.

HOW DO YOU EAT
AN ELEPHANT?
ONE BITE
AT A TIME

ACTIVITY

In the space below, list all of the actions you think you might need to take to achieve your champy. Yes, every single one of them - no matter how big, small, crazy or simple.

GET IT OUT OF YOUR HEAD

AND ONTO THE PAPER.

Now, after you've written your list, I want you to look at it again. Do any steps feel really overwhelming?

CIRCLE THEM, AND THEN ON THE NEXT PAGE

BREAK THEM DOWN INTO EVEN SMALLER STEPS.

FOR EXAMPLE:

Maybe one of your steps is to get some English tutoring, but first you might need to speak to your parents, research tutors, meet with your English teacher, then choose a tutor. You get the idea?

Use the space below to help you break down the overwhelming steps into smaller, more manageable ones.

IMPORTANT:

Not everything on your list will help you to achieve your champy.
So, for example, maybe you go to English tutoring, but after three months your marks haven't improved.
That's ok! You can let it go and try something else.
The rule is: Try it! If it works, great, if it doesn't – hey, at least you gave it a crack!

GIVING UP
ON YOUR GOAL
BECAUSE YOU
HAD A SETBACK
IS LIKE SLASHING
YOUR OTHER THREE
TYRES BECAUSE
YOU HAD A FLAT

Most of the times I've set a goal for myself, I haven't achieved it and I end up feeling like a failure. I see you do really cool things, like Ironman, and it seems like you can achieve anything! Is that just because of who you are, or is there something else that helps you achieve your goals?

— Melinda, 15

A

This is such a huge q because I've actually spent a lot of time trying to understand my own goal getting methods. I've even developed a whole course about it (it's called School of Champions) – in fact, that's where the word champy comes from!

I've created a brief overview of my seven steps to champy chasing success, but before we get to that, there's something I really want to address first:

There have been plenty of things that I just haven't achieved.

In fact, there's a whole list of things that I still want to do but, for whatever reason, I just haven't been able to summon the energy and dedication required to achieve them yet. The bottom line is, achieving a champy involves a stack of hard work and commitment. It's not easy to achieve a champy and failure is often a big part of the process. In fact, it's a really important part, because it teaches you so much.

So don't get hung up on the stuff you haven't achieved. Focus on all the things you have achieved.

And don't waste another minute thinking you have to be a certain type of person to be successful! You might see pics of me crossing that Ironman finish line, but you don't see all the times I've tried, and failed, to play the harp . Be kind to yourself and remind yourself that if you're not failing, it means your probably staying inside your comfort zone, instead of stretching yourself outside it. Failure is a good thing! And, as promised, here are my seven steps to help you chase down those big dreams of yours.

GET YOUR GOAL: STEPS TO GOAL-GETTING SUCCESS

1

How do I love me?

Spend some time getting clear on who you are. Stay in touch with the things that fuel you – the things you love to do. These are the things that will drive your success.

2

Clarity creates power

Get clear and super specific about what you want and, more importantly, WHY you want it.

3

Break those barriers

Try to anticipate all the obstacles that stand between you and your goal and find ways to overcome them. Don't be surprised if the biggest obstacle is, you guessed it, you! Practise turning the volume down on your internal critic.

4

Success is a team effort

Cultivate a kickass crew – this means surrounding yourself with driven and like-minded people.

5

Baby steps, baby!

It's great to know where you're going and what you want BUT it's easy to give up when you just focus on the long game. Focus on taking baby steps.

6

Look after yourself

You're gonna need a solid foundation to work from – this means healthy body, healthy mind. Prioritise your health, always.

7

Stick to it

Champions in any field have made a habit of doing what others find boring or uncomfortable. It's not what we do every now and then that makes a difference – it's what we do day in and day out that makes a difference. Consistency is key.

Don't want to go it alone? You and I can smash your goals together in School of Champions.

turiaschampions.com

I set a goal for myself this year to run a 5 km race but I feel kind of stupid because all my friends are training for a 14 km run. My goal seems really silly in comparison. Should I just train for the 14 km race instead?

— Bella, 17

A

Bella, this is such a good question, and it's something that comes up all the time for people inside my course, School of Champions.

First of all, it's important that we always work towards champies that really stretch us out of our comfort zone, because it's only out of our comfort zones that we really grow.

But you've gotta do you. So, if running a 5 km race is truly a stretch for you, then hell yeah! Make that your champy and don't be swayed by what other people are doing.

Comparing yourself to what you used to be able to do, what someone else is doing, or what you think you should be doing doesn't help you to feel good about yourself and the progress you're making.

So, pick a champy that will drive you and stick to it!

If, on the other hand, you're already running 3-4 km really easily, then maybe running a 5 km race isn't a big enough stretch for you.

If that's the case, choose a champy that does feel like a big stretch and go for that. It might be a 10 k, or a 14 k. Hell, you might even take on a half marathon!

Remember – if you're not finding the process challenging, then it's not forcing you to grow ... and that, my friend, is not a champy worthy of you.

ONE MORE THING:

I know it's not easy to stop comparing yourself to what you used to be able to do, what someone else is doing or what you think you should be doing.

Trust me, I know exactly how hard it is when you feel like your champies and your progress just don't stack up. In hospital I had to completely adjust the bar for what I could achieve. I couldn't even walk, let alone run an ultra-marathon, like I was used to doing.

That was really, really hard for me and it took me a while to adjust. Every time I hit a new milestone, say walking 5 metres, I'd be happy, but part of me would compare myself to what I used to be able to do and I'd think I was so pathetic.

It made me feel so bad, and that's when I realised I had to stop comparing myself to what I used to do. I learnt to focus only on the progress I was making week to week and month to month.

It was the same when I was training for Ironman.

There would be days when I'd feel like, despite all my work, sweat and tears, I just wasn't getting anywhere. But then I'd pull out old training plans and see that, actually I had improved!

Progress is progress, no matter how small.

Always measure your progress against how far you've come already, not on what others are doing or what you think you 'should' be able to do.

Photo credit: Michael Klein

DON'T WAIT
UNTIL YOU'VE
REACHED YOUR
GOAL TO BE PROUD
OF YOURSELF—
BE PROUD OF
EVERY STEP YOU
TAKE TOWARD
REACHING
THAT GOAL

PROGRESS IS SOMETIMES MEASURED IN MILLIMETRES BUT PROGRESS IS PROGRESS, NO MATTER HOW SMALL

TL;DR

1	When you set a champy – one that scares you and excites you and pushes you way outside your comfort zone – and then you do the work to achieve it, you learn a whole heap about yourself. Your confidence skyrockets, your resilience deepens and you develop an ability to overcome all kinds of challenges. Yes please!
2	Ask WHY. Having a compelling reason for achieving your champy will help motivate you to get there.
3	Focus on taking baby steps.
4	Only compare your progress to how far you've come. Don't compare yourself to other people or what you think you 'should' be doing.
5	Do you! Achieving a champy = lots of hard work. If you're gonna get through the grind, it should be for something that really matters to YOU, not anyone else.

Remember: progress is progress, no matter how small.

HARD TIMES

HARD TIMES

As you probably know, I travel a lot for work, giving motivational speeches around the country. At every event, there's someone who will come up to me quietly and ask how I can be so positive. They'll say things like: 'I could never get through something like that. I'd probably just curl up and avoid the world.'

Yes, what happened to me was tough. Emotionally and physically. And I could've very easily lived out the rest of my life like a hermit – and no one would blame me.

But, here's the thing: we all face challenges in our life. All of us are gonna face times that are stressful and hard.

EVEN WHEN YOU
GET AN F FOR
THE SITUATION
ITSELF, YOU CAN
STILL EARN AN A++
FOR HOW YOU
DEAL WITH IT

— SHERYL SANDBERG

Part of living is accepting that there are gonna be things in life that we'd rather not face. Very often, those things will be completely outside our control.

You might struggle with some subjects at school. Maybe your parents will go through a divorce, maybe you or a family member will face a serious illness. You might have to face the death of someone you love.

But while we can't always control what challenges us, we can control how we choose to respond. I truly believe that life is 10% what happens to us and 90% how we react. In the next few q + a's I'll share some of the tools I use when facing tough times.

LIFE:

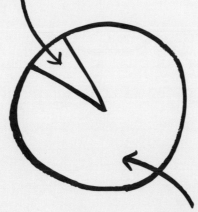

10% WHAT HAPPENS TO US

90% HOW WE REACT

Q

Has having a positive outlook affected the way you got through your recovery?

— Lachlan, 17

A

Yes, 100%.

(Geez, this book would be a lotttttt shorter if I just answered every question like that!)

I remember this day, early in my recovery, when I was really struggling to come to terms with what had happened to me. One of my favourite nurses gave me some great advice.

She said 'Turia, you've gotta focus on what you CAN do; stop focusing on all the things you can't do'.

She was right. Instead of getting upset because I couldn't do something yet, I started looking at what I could do.

I still do this today. Whenever I get upset because I can't do something, I focus on all the things I can do. I can run my own business, I can surf, I can raise millions of dollars for Interplast, I'm compassionate, I have determination by the truckload ... and you know what's really awesome? I can do things that some able-bodied people can't do. I mean, I've done Kona, one of the toughest endurance races in the world! It doesn't benefit me to think about the things I can't do so I always try to keep the focus on what I can do.

This idea forms the basis of one of my favourite tools for changing the way I view challenges:

REFRAMING

Nope, I'm not suddenly selling myself as an interior designer! I'm not talking about the pictures on your walls, I'm talking about reframing the way you see your challenges, your life and your champies.

In a nutshell, reframing means looking at the same situation in a different way.

I do this all the time.

I'll give you an example ...

The challenge I'm facing:

Every year, I have about four operations. No one looks forward to surgery and, even after having over 200 medical procedures, it's still not easy.

Option One

Looking at it through the negative frame:

It's scary, it's painful, there are no guarantees as to what the outcome will look and feel like, you lose a lot of time in recovery and you can't really do that much. So, it's easy for me to feel down because I can't go outside for a run or go down to the ocean for a surf – the stuff I do to help me feel good.

It can also be hard to keep working towards your goals when you've got to take a few weeks out. If I looked at the operations like this, there's no way I'd want to do them!

Option Two

Looking at operations through the positive frame:

I get to catch up with all the medical staff who have worked with me over the years, it's a forced time out and a break from work, I get to eat ice cream 🍦 and watch as many movies as I want to, I can spend all day in my pyjamas, I get a lot of visits from my friends and family, if I want to improve myself this is part of the deal, how lucky am I that I live in Australia and that if I want an operation, I can speak to my doctors and make it happen!

If I look at my operations like this, I look forward to them. It makes me feel grateful to live in Australia and it helps me understand that surgery, for me, is part of the process of improving myself.

REFRAMING

ONE

You ready to give it a shot? Now I've talked up the magic of reframing; Think of a situation that might stress you out.

E.g. spraining your ankle mid-footy season.

WRITE IT DOWN:
_____

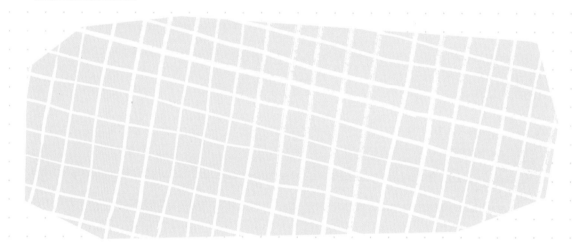

TWO

NOW, WRITE DOWN ALL OF THE
_____
NEGATIVE STUFF THAT MIGHT
_____
HAPPEN IF THAT SITUATION
_____
BECAME TRUE. LIST ABSOLUTELY
_____
EVERY FEAR OR WORRY YOU HAVE.
_____

E.g. I'd let the team down, all my hard work at training would be for nothing, I'd be devastated I couldn't play with my mates every weekend. Go crazy in negative land here, on the facing page.

THREE

NOW, WRITE DOWN ALL
_____
THE POSITIVE STUFF THAT
_____
MIGHT HAPPEN.
_____

E.g. I might have more free time to work on my guitar practice. I'd have fewer distractions for my study and homework. I might be able to work with the coaches as an assistant and learn about coaching.

NEGATIVE

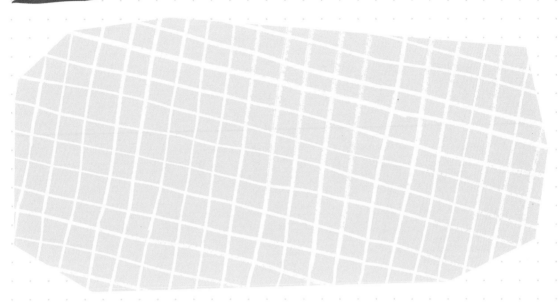

POSITIVE

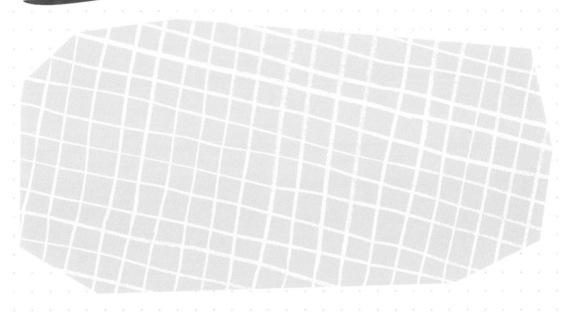

Now, you have a choice. You can look at things in the worst way or you can look at them in the best way. It's up to you.

Q

Do you still have hard times? If you do, what do you do to manage them?

— Emily, 14

A

Yep, of course. But everyone does. Bad days and hard times are part of life. Remember #AllTheEmojis? (Turn to page 76 if you've got no idea what I'm talking about!)

Just because I went through a really tough time after the fire, it doesn't mean my life is always easy now.

Below is a quick list of some hard times I've faced in life so far:

— I had bad eczema at school and got teased for it

— I was in a bus crash coming home from school and one of our classmates died

— I went to three different high schools in three years and got 'asked to leave' at one of the schools

— My parents had to sell their house because they couldn't afford the mortgage repayments

— My parents divorced when I was in high school

— I was told by my teacher that I wasn't smart enough to get the grades I wanted

— My father-in-law got really sick

— At university, I had a mean, controlling boyfriend who made my confidence hit rock bottom

— On my first day studying Engineering at uni, classmates told me I didn't belong, because I was a girl in a male-dominated class

— I got catastrophically injured during the ultra marathon

— I got made redundant from my job

— I had to endure a court case that went on for years

— One of the surviving runners from the fire, Martin Van De Merwe, died while he was training for an adventure race

I'm not saying this stuff to make you feel sorry for me.
I'm just trying to emphasise that bad stuff happens
to all of us - all of us go through tough and hard times.

Maybe a family member has cancer, maybe you've had
a falling out with a friend, maybe you're getting bullied
at school.

But the important thing to remember is that these tough
times make you STRONGER.

Each time I go through a tough time in my life now, I think
'I've had tough times before, and I've survived them -
I'm gonna survive this one too'.

ACTIVITY

I'd love you to have a think about the hard times you've got through.

These don't have to be BIG things either. If you struggled with maths last year, write that down! If you found it tough breaking up with your boyfriend or girlfriend, write it down. If you had a fight with a friend, write it down.

WRITE THEM IN THE SPACE BELOW

Now, the next time you feel like life is getting hard, look back at this list and remember that you're a badass, strong, powerful person who has got through all kinds of tough times before.

Remember, you're the boss of you. You're always in control of how you respond to challenges.

Q

What do you do to be able to remain happy after what has happened?

— Chloe, 11

A

I think there's this idea out there that we are supposed to be happy all the time. I don't think that's possible. You know, we are gonna have bad days and mediocre days too. We're not always gonna be super pumped about life!

But, and it's a big but, YOU are in charge of your own happiness.

That doesn't mean it's easy! Sometimes I'll wake up in the morning and won't feel really happy. I don't feel inspired or motivated or excited every day. You know, I might not want to get out of bed or I might be dreading a tough phone call I need to make.

On those days I say to myself 'Are you gonna let today be a bad day or are you gonna choose to make today a brilliant day?' (refer to my bad days flowchart link on page 19).

Some days I might go 'Yeah actually, I'm gonna make today awesome!' and I'll turn things around. But some days I think 'You know what, I don't have the energy to make it into a good day; today might just need to be average'. That's ok.

I'm not saying you always have to be happy – but you do get to change it if you're not.

That's cool Turia, but how do I do that?

—

Well, I've created a list of things that help me boost my happy levels.

I call it my Happy Bank.

You can create one too.

TURIA'S HAPPY BANK

For me, that includes:

getting outside for a surf or bushwalk, reading a good book or watching a good movie (check out my list of faves on page 165), practising gratitude, giving back or volunteering, spending time with friends and planning exciting holidays or events to look forward to.

HAPPY BANK

In the space below, write down all the things that make you feel good about life.

WHAT CAN YOUR LIST INCLUDE?

Maybe you like listening to music, riding your bike or going to the beach?

WRITE YOUR IDEAS BELOW

Next time you don't feel so crash hot, try picking something from your Happy Bank to go and do.

Remember - you're in charge of your own happiness!

YO, THIS IS IMPORTANT

Ever wondered why everyone talks about exercise as a great way to help you feel more positive about life? Well, there's a reason for that.

See, when you move your body (say, going for a walk, taking a dance class etc), your body makes more norepinephrine. No, that's not a typo! Norepinephrine is a chemical that can help your brain respond to stress better. When you exercise your brain also releases more endorphins and dopamine - two chemicals that make you feel good.

INTERESTED IN LEARNING MORE ABOUT FEEL-GOOD CHEMICALS + HOW TO GET THEM?

Some basic info below:

CHEMICAL	WHAT IT DOES	HOW TO USE TO YOUR ADVANTAGE
ENDORPHINS	Masks physical pain. Chemically similar to morphine.	Want to increase your endorphins? Laugh really hard or do some exercise. Endorphins are what runners call the 'runner's high' – it makes them feel great!
DOPAMINE	Boosts our drive, focus and concentration.	There's a lot of ways you can boost your dopamine - such as eating the right foods (hello bananas!), physical exercise, and meditation. Also, the harder you work to achieve something, the more dopamine you'll get when you achieve it. Cool!
SEROTONIN	This is that feeling of pride — the feeling we get when we feel that others like us and respect us. Serotonin makes us feel strong and confident - often referred to as the 'mood' drug.	You can boost your serotonin by getting some sun, by exercising, and reflecting on happy events.
OXYTOCIN	This is what makes you feel all warm and fuzzy when you're spending time with people you love. It's because of oxytocin we feel human connections.	Oxytocin is all about human touch and connection, so try boosting it by hugging a family member or close friend, giving compliments, and smiling and laughing with your mates.

WHAT SEEMS IMPOSSIBLE TODAY WILL ONE DAY BE YOUR WARM-UP

TL;DR

1	Everyone has hard times, including me and you. But while we can't always control what happens to us, we do get to choose how we respond.
2	Try reframing a 'bad' situation.
3	Focus on what you can do instead of what you can't do.
4	Try out my list of things that make me happy, and add some of your own. Practise them regularly!

6

GOT SUP— PORT?

Something I know for sure is that success is always a team effort. There's no way I would have been able to achieve everything I have since the fire without the team of people around me.

I've had the help of brilliant surgeons and nurses who helped save my life, physios and coaches who helped me train for Ironman, and a whole bunch of people supporting me behind the scenes.

PLUS I've had two people who never stopped believing – my partner Michael and my mum.

When it comes to any challenge or any champy you're taking on, a kickass support team is CRUCIAL.

But what if you don't feel like you've got the right support?

Well, in this chapter, I'm answering some of the most common q's I get asked about this. Read on!

Q

What would be your advice for someone who doesn't feel like they can get through a hard time on their own?

— Pat, 16

A

Pat, my advice is simple: it's ok to ask for help.
I'm gonna say that again, and in a bigger font:

It's ok to ask for help.

Just as I had to get a team of surgeons and doctors helping me physically, I knew I needed help on the emotional and mental side as well.

My psychologist (like a doctor who studies our brain – how we think, feel and behave) was a really big part of my recovery process.

She helped me find ways to get through all the hard stuff I was facing. Asking for that help was one of the best things I've ever done.

Yes, it was really hard opening up to a perfect stranger! But remember, you're in the driver's seat. The first couple of sessions, I didn't even say that much. But gradually, over months, we built up a rapport and I felt like I could start opening up to her.

If you're having a hard time, feeling anxious or sad or worried all the time, please go and talk to someone. There's zero shame in sharing how you're feeling with someone you trust.

If you don't have someone at home you can talk to, try a teacher, a counsellor, psychologist or doctor or an adult you trust.
See page 19 for some links to resources you can try.

THE MOST IMPORTANT RELATIONSHIP YOU'LL EVER HAVE IS THE ONE YOU HAVE WITH YOURSELF

— DIANE VON FURSTENBERG

This is really important: if you go to one person and they don't help you in the way you need, try someone else.

I know it's scary to talk about the things that worry you, and I know just talking to one person about it is a big step.

But you might not find the right person straight away. And that's ok. You will find the right person; it might just involve trying a few times.

I tried a few different counsellors and psychologists before I found the right one.

Finding the right psychologist is a little bit like trying to find a comfy pair of shoes ... you have to try on a few, and even go for a walk in a few pairs, before you find the perfect one.

So, never be afraid to ask for help.

You're not weak for needing a hand; you're brave for asking for it.

PS – Check out these cool animals helping each other out on the link on page 19.

Q

I really want to go to university but my grades haven't been very good. On top of that, no one in my family has ever been to uni before. My parents think it might be better if I did some other kind of training at TAFE and then get straight into a job. How do I get them on board with my dream?

— Melissa, 17

A

Ah, families can be tricky can't they?!

Sometimes it feels like family can be the biggest doubters of our dreams. I'm sure they're not trying to hurt you by suggesting another path; it's maybe just that they're too close to the situation and just want to look out for you.

When I bit the bullet and signed up for Ironman, my mum was worried. She thought it would be too much for my body. My dad thought I would get too cold in the swim and Michael wondered what I was trying to prove. It's not that they thought I couldn't or wouldn't do it. They were just concerned for me.

Here's what you need to do:

Sit your parents down and explain to them, really clearly, why you want to go to university so much.

Be as prepared for this conversation as possible.

Show them the game plan you have in place to get the marks you need. Show them that you've thought about how you'll be able to afford to go and the steps you'll take to make that happen.

By having an honest conversation with them, you're showing that you're committed to this champy and that you have given a lot of thought to how you're going to achieve it.

That should help them jump on board with your dreams.

This works for any champy - not just wanting to go to university.

If there's something you really want to work towards but your friends or family aren't supportive - chat to them about it.

Show them that you're committed by talking through your game plan and be honest about the reasons why you want it.

That said, be aware that you're not always going to have everyone's support. You can show them your plan, you can tell them how committed you are BUT you can't always change people's minds.

That's ok.

The only way you can avoid doubt and criticism throughout your whole life is to do nothing, say nothing and be nothing.

ONE MORE THING:

It's not just your family who can be doubtful. Your friends play a part too. So, here's a q for you: are your friends supportive of you? Reflect on how you feel about yourself after you've hung out with your friends. Do they help you to feel confident, brave and positive, and like you're capable of achieving your dreams? Or do they put you down? If a friend isn't being supportive, remember that you get to choose who you spend your time with. You don't need to hang out with people who bring you down.

People will try and tell you that you're too young, too old, too smart, too dumb or too lazy to achieve your dreams, but remember: opinions are like belly buttons. We've all got 'em!

People doubt and criticise for different reasons. It might be because they're genuinely concerned (yes, if you go to uni, you might find it hard to pay your rent some weeks).

It might be because seeing people achieve massive goals in their life can make them feel inadequate.

The bottom line is, when you're on your way to creating something new in your life, there's gonna be doubters, like it or not.

Incidentally, the only people who can offer you real insights into what you want to achieve are those who have either done it or are currently doing it.

These people are the ones you should listen to, not your Uncle Gary who has never left the state of South Australia!

As always, you do you.

Q

I don't have a very wide circle of friends. What can I do?

—Emily, 14

A

Well, I would say that when it comes to friends it's always quality over quantity. You are the average of the five people you spend the most time with.

So, if you hang around with intelligent, funny, brave and kind people, they probably help you to be more intelligent, funny, brave and kind yourself.

I know you can't always control who you spend most of your time with. But I do know that when you hang out with people who make you feel good, life is infinitely better.

It doesn't matter if you don't have heaps of friends. Focus on forming close friendships with people you really like. People whose values you admire, people who challenge you to be better and people who make you laugh!

My biggest tip for creating new friendships is to be the person you want to spend time with. So, if you want funny, intelligent and brave friends? Well, guess who's gonna be cracking jokes while diving with sharks 🦈 on a marine biology expedition? You are! Haha!

No, what I mean is that you've gotta put yourself out there in new ways, doing the things you love to do.

So, if you want to meet outdoorsy, nature-loving friends, join a local trail running or hiking club. If you want to meet geology nerds (that's me, I'm a rock geek!), maybe you can save up to go to a geology camp next summer.

Think outside the box and always be the person YOU want to spend time with.

Q

Did you lose any friends after the fire?

—Haelie, 13

A

Yeah, I did actually. It was really upsetting.

You know, a crazy, unbelievable, life changing thing happened to me and a lot of my friends didn't know what to say or how to handle it. It was pretty hard to deal with at the time.

Now I know that when your friends go through hard times, it's really important to let them know that you're there for them.

I know that it can be awkward when a friend is having a tough time, or experiencing grief or loss. Like, what do you even say??

Well, you say 'I don't know what to say ... but I know this is a really hard time for you and I'm here for you'.

I love these empathy cards designed by Emily McDowell (see link on page 19). Sometimes, when you don't know what words to say to someone, it's ok to just give them a card that says 'I know this day really sucks for you'.

Make time and space for your friends. Don't be offended if they don't take you up on your offers to hang out. Just keep letting them know that you're around and you'll be there.

It's really that simple.

If you want more info on how to help someone going through a hard time, check out the Kvetching Circle (see link on page 19).

IMPORTANT

When it comes to wanting help from your friends and family, it's important that you lead by example.

If a friend or family member needs your help, get on board! If your younger brother asks for help with his homework, then bust out a red pen and start helping him ASAP.

Show your loved ones that you're as invested in their champies as they are in yours. After all, you can't expect the people around you to help out if you're not helping back!

TL;DR

1	Sometimes we don't get the support we were hoping for from our friends and family. When this happens, talk to them about why their support matters to you.
2	It's ok to ask for help.
3	But remember, you're not always going to have everyone's support, and that's ok. You've gotta do you.
4	Be the person YOU want to spend time with.
5	When a friend is having a hard time, be there for them. If you don't know what to say, try 'I don't know what to say, but I'm here for you'.

PERSPECTIVE

7

GET A LITTLE PERSP— ECTIVE

You know when you feel a bit stuck in your life? Like, all you can see in your life is what's wrong with it?

Don't stress. We all feel that way sometimes and I've got the antidote to feeling that way.

All you need is a little dose of something called perspective.

See, when we only focus on our own lives, we tend to become self absorbed and then it's easy to only see what's wrong with us. And then our problems can seem bigger and harder than they really are.

But when you find a new way of looking at the world, aka a new perspective, you'll start to see your problems in a different way too!

Give back

—

Giving back and helping others is the main way I help myself to get some perspective and see the bigger picture of life.

I've always thought it was important to help others. Throughout school and uni, I raised money for a few different charities. I even rode my bike across Cambodia to raise money for a charity called ChildFund.

Those experiences gave me a lot of perspective and really changed how I saw myself and the world. It made me realise that my life was pretty bloody amazing and helped me to feel gratitude for all the opportunities provided to me in Australia.

So, if you ever find yourself feeling really 'ugh', find a way to give back. Help a neighbour, support a cause you care about, volunteer in your community.

You'll get a huge hit of perspective – the way you see your life and your problems will dramatically start to change and you'll start to see the whole world in a different way.

Yew! That's a really good thing!

Q

After your experiences, what made you want to go and help others when you yourself were still recovering?

— Monique, 14

After I'd been in hospital a few months I kept noticing that one of my surgeons would disappear for a few weeks at a time. I assumed he was taking off on fancy holidays to tropical islands so, when I next saw him, I teasingly asked why he didn't have a better tan after being on holiday so much!

He told me that he'd actually been volunteering with a charity called Interplast.

In a nutshell, Interplast sends teams of Australian doctors, surgeons, nurses, physios and all kinds of medical professionals to poor or developing countries.

The Aussie medical teams perform free surgery on patients who need it and then help to train local doctors and medical staff in that country. So they might help kids with cleft lip and cleft palate, women who've had acid thrown on their face and even other burn survivors.

But I became really interested in Interplast and I knew I wanted to help in any way I could.

I also knew that giving back in some way would not only help others, it would also help me get some perspective on my own situation.

Before the fire ...

—

... I felt so blessed to live in Australia but it was only afterwards that I realised how bloody lucky we are to live here.

If my accident had happened in a developing country, there's no question –

I would have died.

Access to quality medical care is one of those things you don't think about much and take for granted until you really need it.

I've been an Ambassador for Interplast since about 2013 and I'm really proud to have helped raise over one million dollars for them since then.

WE MAKE
A LIVING BY
WHAT WE GET,
BUT WE MAKE
A LIFE BY WHAT
WE GIVE

— WINSTON CHURCHILL

Q

Last year I raised $115 for a cancer charity. I'm proud of myself for trying but it doesn't feel like that's enough to even make a difference. Did you ever feel this way when you started fundraising?

— Ella, 16

A

Ella, yes, I really did feel this way when I first started fundraising!

I first did the 40-hour famine when I was really young. I worked really hard to raise money and when the famine was over, I'd managed to raise a few hundred dollars. I remember saying to my mum: 'It's not enough. How will this even make a difference?'

My mum's answer has stayed with me to this day. She told me this quote:

'If you think you're too small to make a difference, try sleeping with a mosquito.'

You're never too small or too young to make a difference. It doesn't matter how old you are, you can always find a way to help someone else; even if you only help one person, I think that person will tell you it's worth it!

Remember, even the smallest act of charity can have an enormous ripple effect – impacting more people than you might even realise.

There's another way I get some perspective.

Whenever I feel like my problems are just too huge, I turn to books. Yep, I pick up books written by people who have overcome really big obstacles, or books about the way people live in different parts of the world.

I also watch docos about the planet and historical movies. It helps me get a fresh perspective on the world and helps me to see my own problems in a different way.

In fact, one of the first things I did after the fire was ask Michael to bring me any books or movies he could find about people who had been through life changing events and come out the other side stronger than before.

Knowing other people have faced tough times gave me a new perspective.

I knew that if others had done it, I could do it too.

Even now, when I feel like things are hard in my work or business, I read books about people who have built companies from the ground up. It helps me to see that, really, anything is possible.

So, if you feel like you need a fresh perspective, hit up iBooks or your local library or bookshop and get reading. Not a reader? No worries. Watch some docos on Netflix or YouTube! Check out some of my fave books and movies on the facing page.

ONE MORE THING:

Just as it's important to watch and read inspirational stories to get a different perspective on life, it's also important to surround yourself with people who are positive and supportive.

When you hang out with people who are critical or closed minded, that can limit how you see the world too.

Keep your inner circle full of open, positive and big-minded people! Turn to page 138 for more tips on how to form your crew.

Books and movies

—

I encourage you to read and watch stories about different kinds of people and different kinds of lives. Seeing the world through someone else's eyes will give you a fresh perspective on your own life.

Below is a list of books and movies I recommend for whenever you feel like life is getting too hard. These helped me, and I'm sure they can help you too!

COOL BOOKS

— *Head Over Heels* by Sam Bailey
— *Never Tell Me Never* by Janine Shepherd
— *Don't Die with the Music in You* by Wayne Bennett
— *Pushing the Limits* by Kurt Fearnley
— *Soul Surfer* by Bethany Hamilton
— *Good Night Stories for Rebel Girls* by Elena Favilli and Francesca Cavallo
— *True Spirit* by Jessica Watson
— *Wonder* by R. J. Palacio
— *The Girl Who Climbed Everest* by Alyssa Azar
— *Into Thin Air* by Jon Krakauer
— *The Happiest Refugee* by Anh Do

COOL MOVIES

— The Blind Side
— Million Dollar Baby
— My Left Foot
— Good Will Hunting
— The Shawshank Redemption
— Forrest Gump
— Erin Brockovich
— A Beautiful Mind
— The Diving Bell and the Butterfly
— The Intouchables (French film)
— Cool Runnings
— Touching the Void
— Mulan
— Remember the Titans
— Pay It Forward
— October Sky

NOTE:

Make sure you grab Mum or Dad's ok before you read these books or watch these movies. Also, check out this funny clip about first world problems (see page 19 for the link).

IF YOU THINK YOU'RE TOO SMALL TO MAKE A DIFFERENCE, TRY SLEEPING WITH A MOSQUITO

— DALAI LAMA

TL;DR

1	When you only focus on your own life, your problems instantly seem bigger and harder than they really are.
2	Getting a new perspective on life is the antidote to feeling this way.
3	Giving back and helping others is a great way to get perspective.
4	Remember, you're never too small to make a difference.
5	If in doubt, read, read, read! Read all kinds of books about people facing challenges and living lives different from yours.

I AM
NOT WHAT
HAPPENED
TO ME,

I AM WHAT
I CHOOSE
TO BECOME

— CARL JUNG

THAT'S A WRAP!

It feels like it might be time to wrap things up. Yes, my friend, the end (of this book) is near! I hope that you've picked up some cool ideas along the way – some strategies and tools for creating your good selfie.

You know, answering all of these q's was an interesting experience for me. It helped me to reflect on all the lessons I've learned through my childhood, my time at uni, the fire, recovery from the fire, my re-invention from Mining Engineer to athlete, author and mindset coach, all the hard stuff I've faced, and all the moments of joy and happiness and success.

I've learnt that the relationship you have with yourself is the most important relationship you'll have, that tough times make you stronger, and that you can do anything when you have the support of people who lift you up.

I've learnt that chasing champies makes you more confident and more resilient, that giving back shapes how you see the world and your life, and that confidence comes from a lot more than just what you look like.

All of these lessons form my guide to a good selfie. But all of these little lessons can be hard to remember. So, before I leave you, I want to answer one last question.

It comes from Douglas, aged 17:

Q

What actually matters in life?

— Douglas, 17

A

Douglas, this q is EPIC.

See, in the years since my accident, this is something I've thought about a lot, and while I think everyone will answer this question a little differently, there are three things that I believe really matter to everyone:

ONE We need to feel like we're making progress – like we're working towards something that is important to us.

TWO We need to have strong relationships with people who make us feel good.

THREE We want to feel happy and confident about ourselves.

To me, these three things sum up all of the lessons I've shared in this book.

It's a quick and simple checklist for you to keep in mind as you go through life's ups and downs.

If you're moving towards the things you want, if you're surrounded by people who lift you up, and if you're working on feeling confident, happy and strong – well, that's when your life is gonna have purpose and meaning.

So, let's talk about you

—

Yes, you reading this book.

I know that you want to live a life that is big and full and completely on your own terms – not how your parents, teachers or friends want it to be, but how YOU want it to be.

I get it. That's what I'm all about.

I want you to know that you have it within you to create that life.

Going out of your way to find this book, reading it and taking some of my strategies on board shows me that you're gonna make it happen.

So, now it's over to you.

I want to challenge you to set champies that excite you; to trust that, while failure and hard times are inevitable, they're gonna make you stronger and smarter; to surround yourself with great people; and to know that your confidence is something that you can build.

I have a feeling you're gonna do incredible things. Now it's up to you to prove me right.

I'd bloody love that.

TURIA xx

Mental health resources

—

As I say in this book, if you're having a hard time or maybe feeling anxious or depressed, I really encourage you to seek support.

My psychologist was instrumental in my recovery process and it's always ok to ask for help.

I've listed some Australian resources that you can use to get started here:

HEADSPACE

The national youth mental health foundation dedicated to improving the wellbeing of young Australians
Visit headspace.org.au or call 1800 650 890.

REACHOUT

ReachOut.com helps under 25s get through everything from everyday issues to tough times.
Visit ReachOut.com.

LIFELINE

Crisis support and suicide prevention.
Visit lifeline.org.au or call 13 11 14.

Acknowledgements

—

As I mention in this book, nothing is ever achieved alone. I work with an extraordinary team who helped me put this book together. Thank you Grace McBride, Kristen Tonkin, Amanda Whitty and Melissa Clorley – I appreciate and value everything you do for Team Turia!

A round of thank yous must also go to the book design team – Freda, Evi and Su – you interpreted my vague brief and created something magical. It was an honour to work with pros like you!

Thanks also to Luke Vandenbergh from Moss Vale High School for his insights, and for Eliza Vassallo for reviewing this book.

Finally, a big thank you to my beautiful Hakavai – you're keeping your mum young at heart.

ABOUT THE TEAM

TURIA

Turia Pitt is living proof that, with the right mindset, anything is possible. Caught in a grassfire while competing in a 100 km ultramarathon in 2011, Turia suffered full thickness burns to 65% of her body. But surviving is the least of her achievements. One of Australia's most admired and widely recognised people, Turia has gone on to become a bestselling author, two-time Ironman and humanitarian - raising well over a million dollars for not-for-profit Interplast. Through her online presence, books and online programs, Turia has inspired millions to live with more confidence, drop their fears and smash epic goals.

turiapitt.com / @turiapitt

FREDA

Freda Chiu is an independent illustrator and visual artist from Sydney, Australia. She creates art notably for books, editorial and comics. As well as illustrating, Freda lectures on Illustration and Animation Design at the University of Technology, Sydney.

fredachiu.com / @_fredachiu_

EVI-O STUDIO

Evi-O Studio is an award-winning, multi-disciplinary and collaborative design practice working both locally and internationally across publishing, branding and beyond. We are a small team of passionate creatives who believe in creating thoughtful and engaging design that elevates the impact of each and every project. In short, we are weird nerds who never know what to eat for lunch but love reading, 3 pm dance offs and Henri (our office pup).

evi-o.studio / @evi_o_studio

Published in 2019 by Vahine Press (an imprint of Renniks Publications)

 A catalogue record for this
book is available from the
National Library of Australia

Good Selfie: Tips & Tools for Teens to Nail Life
ISBN: 978 0 9871057 4 5

Author: Turia Pitt
Illustrations: Freda Chiu
Cover Design: Evi O Studio / Evi O & Susan Le
Internal Design: Evi O Studio / Susan Le
Editor: Rachel Carter
Publisher: Vahine Press (an imprint of Renniks Publciations)
Printed and bound in China by 1010

RENNIKS
PUBLICATIONS